How to Coach a Debate Team

Thomas Jerome Baker

Copyright © 2012 Thomas Jerome Baker
All rights reserved.
ISBN: 1477532358
ISBN-13: 978-1477532355

DEDICATION

This book is dedicated to my family, and their families, and their families yet to be. On countless occasions I've said to them:

"One day I will write our story."

This time it is I who again make the promise, "One day, I will write our story". Like all writers, I have no clue if the promise will ever be kept, yet I must admit, I enjoy writing for you.

More importantly, I have the aspiration that you will find things in my writing with which you can identify.

In this way, you my brother, Charlie, and you, my sisters, Linda, Kathy and Bernice, will become heirs to a shared memory of days gone by, days present, and days yet to come. More importantly, the memory will live beyond us, beyond our days, and beyond our time. And that is well as it should be.

Thus, this is the reason I write for you.

Again, it has been my pleasure to write the treasured and shared memory, my teacher story, for you.

CONTENTS

	Acknowledgments	i
1	Debating In The Classroom	1
2	What Does A Debate Coach Do?	14
3	Gender Equality Debate	18
4	Definitions First	23
5	The Right to Die	31
6	Death Penalty Debate	34
7	Pro or Contra	38
8	Smoking Should Be Prohibited	48
9	Malcolm X Debates at Oxford	51
10	What Every Debate Coach Should Know	54
	Appendix: This House Believes That	61
	About the Author	62

Preface

Different coaches have different theories about how to coach a successful debate team. As you will find in this book, I believe in understanding debate from the practical side.

In this book, we start our journey with debating in the classroom, where most students encounter debate for the first time. We move on to the moment of shock and surprise when you find out you are the debate coach and need to recruit a debate team.

Then we begin to study debating, through actual debates. We look at the gender equality debate, and after that, look at the importance of definitions. From there, we move on to the right to die debate, for the individual to take his/her own life, and contrast that with the capital punishment debate. Why do we say "Yes" in the one instance and "No" in the other?

We move next to the prohibition of smoking in public places. Do smokers have any rights? Where can you smoke a cigarette nowadays? Then it is off to England, stopping at Oxford, to hear Malcolm X debate the use of extremism to achieve legitimate goals. Finally, a voice from the past century shares information that every debate coach should know.

To wrap things up, the appendix closes with twelve debate motions to keep you supplied with topics to debate. Ultimately, debating helps us to understand how others see the world, and in doing so, creates opportunity for everyone to make a better world, through mutual understanding and tolerance. Debating is what you make of it, in the end. Good luck coach, to you and to your debating team...

ACKNOWLEDGMENTS

This book is inspired by my wife Gabriela, and my son, Thomas Jerome Baker, Jr.

I owe an absolute debt of gratitude for your support and inspiration.

It is you who provide the impetus for me to write, again, and yet again. Thank you, both of you.

I love you both more than words will ever express.

CHAPTER 1

DEBATING IN THE CLASSROOM

"Rhetoric is the art of persuading the minds of men." ~ Plato

By the end of November, 2008, my elementary class of twenty-five (25) 6th-grade boys had finished their textbook and taken the final exams for the 2008 school year. Every student had passed and would be going on to 7th grade. But there were still three more weeks of school left! What could be done to fill the time productively? The purpose of this first chapter is to share with the reader(s) why and how debate was used to resolve this common problem that teachers face.

Why debates?

There were two main reasons. First, various debate activities had been used in the past as a class speaking activity. One favourite is the "Balloon Debate". In this activity, a group of four to eight students is formed. Each student chooses to be a famous person who is in a balloon that is rapidly losing altitude.

The group can only be saved if one person sacrifices themself by jumping overboard. To decide who must jump, each student must give reasons why they should stay in the balloon. The teacher and/or the class (by voting) then decides who has made the least persuasive argument. That person must jump. This process continues until there is only one person left in the balloon, who lands safely, winning the debate.

The second, and most significant, reason for using debates with this class of sixth graders was because of a movie, "The Great Debaters" (2007). It was directed by Denzel Washington. In it Denzel also plays the role of Melvin Tollson, coach of the undefeated Wiley College Debate Team of 1935.

At the beginning of the movie there is a simple yet powerful scene. Denzel is explaining his philosophy about debating. The room is full of nervous students who are trying out for the debate team:

Denzel: "Debate is combat. Your weapons are words. In a debate there is a resolution. One team, called the affirmative team, argues for the resolution.

The other team, called the negative team, argues against the resolution."

That explanation - - clear and direct - - not only clarifies but also inspires. Students eagerly accepted the inherent challenge to "use words as weapons."

Benefits of debating

One major benefit of debating in teams is the collaboration among team members. This social interaction is considered essential by social interactionist theorists, such as Tomasello (2003), Tomasello, Kruger, and Ratner (1993) and Vygotsky (1962, 1978), who state that learning involves the internalization of social interaction processes.

Additionally, other benefits have been claimed. At the 2006 JALT Hokkaido Language Conference a presentation entitled, "*Teaching Debate in the EFL Classroom*", was given by Manning and Nakamura. They have developed a debate course for high school EFL students in Japan. According to Manning and Nakamura:

- Debating ability is a valuable skill.

- Debate utilizes useful English.

- It is a unique way to teach grammar.

- It develops critical thinking skills.

- It introduces global issues.

- It develops research skills.

Let's take a closer look at their ideas, in a general manner. First of all, there can be little doubt that debating is a valuable skill. If we are able to become skilled at presenting our opinions to others, the possible benefits to be gained are almost unlimited. To name only a few: increased self-confidence, making criteria-based decisions, public speaking, and positive interpersonal relationships all come quickly to mind as areas which may be positively affected by gaining the ability to debate.

Secondly, in terms of learning a language, regardless of whether it is a first, second, or foreign language, to participate successfully requires that participants increase their vocabulary. Further, they must also learn to put the vocabulary into expressive forms which can be adapted to a wide variety of speaking situations. In this sense, time spent on debate is well invested.

Thirdly, grammar is being taught coincidentally, embedded into the language that is being used. Grammar is always present, yet the focus is not on learning a particular grammatical item. The focus is on the effective use of English. Therefore, grammar is learned that is needed to accomplish this comunicative goal. This can be thought of as learning grammar naturally, in order to express oneself in a meaningful way that is persuasion oriented.

Fourthly, critical thinking is at the heart of debate. It promotes independent thought processes which seek to understand by examining issues from the standpoint of the evidence that supports a particular position. If the logic and evidence is clear and unequivocal, critical thinking will most likely lead the student to accept a particular position.

On the other hand, if the evidence is not consistent, or is in some way contradictory, the student will most likely reject the position which has been adopted. This way of thinking makes people capable of living in a world that continuously seeks to persuade them to take one decision or another: buying a product, health care, education, automobile, home, vacation, etc.

Fifthly, debating is an excellent platform from which to consider global issues. Nowadays, we live in a globalised world that is interconnected and interdependent. What happens in one part of the world has an almost immediate effect, in one way or another, in another part of the world.

The problems the world is facing are increasingly of such magnitude that solutions require bringing together the best minds, knowledge, skills and abilities of people from a wide diversity of backgrounds in all countries. This requires an awareness of global issues. Debating lends itself well to the examination and discussion of these topics that have global significance.

Finally, research skills are necessary if one is to consider debate topics in any depth. For example, in a debate about using animals for sport and entertainment, it is safe to say that most people do not think that animals should be abused or mistreated. Since this happens in many instances, most inexperienced debaters would not consider doing research.

This would be a fatal mistake, because the opposing team would present a wide variety of factual, statistical, and first-person evidence that would be convincing. To avoid such an outcome, effective research must be undertaken. In sum, to debate effectively, an opinion is not enough. Evidence gained from research must be used to provide clear and compelling support for a particular position.

Why debate?

Next, let's turn to Dr. Alfred Snider, Director of the World Debate Institute at the University of Vermont. He lists six answers to the question, "Why debate?" (Snider, 1999, p.5). They are:

• Debating is fun.

• Debating is a sport of the mind and voice.

• Debating is controlled by you.

• Debating creates the skills you need for success in life.

• Debate can give you the power to change things.

• Debating is not just for "geeks" or "nerds".

Dr. Snider's six reasons present universal truths. Participating in a debate is a way to have good, clean fun. It is the ideas we debate, not the people. It is truth we seek, not manipulation. Matching wits with friends is without a doubt fun for debaters.

Further, it is not enough to use your mind. Logic is necessary, yes, but the voice must be used also. An idea that remains in your mind, and is never voiced, is not helpful to anyone. How do we give voice to our thoughts in such a way that others will pay attention to what we have to say? Debating gives valuable practice in acquiring this essential skill of speaking well in public.

The debater controls the debate. The development of the debate responds to the way that the debaters attempt to prove their ideas. Whether one seeks to employ logic, emotion, or credibility (in the Greek: *Logos, Pathos, Ethos*) or some combination of all these elements of persuasive speech, depends entirely on the strengths and weaknesses of each debater individually, and likewise on the strengths and weaknesses of the team collectively. Let me give an example:

If your team is made up of all boys, it can argue very convincingly for sports in school, based on personal experience. Yet this same team would not be able to argue convincingly to ban beauty contests, as the element of personal experience is not available to them. They would have to seek other sources who are capable of speaking authoritatively on this topic. Hence, the control of the debate is defined by the participants themselves, based on the strategy they choose to use for the debate.

Are debating skills only for academic purposes, useful only in school, without any real world use later in life? The answer is "No". There is an incredibly long list of successful people who participated in debate when they were young. To name only a few:

• Former UN Secretary General **Kofi Annan** competed in the early 60's for Macalester College in St. Paul, Minnesota.

• South African President **Nelson Mandela** debated in college.

• Former British Prime Minister **Margaret Thatcher** competed in debate.

• Former British Prime Minister **John Major** competed in debate.

• President **Lyndon Baines Johnson** taught high school debate.

• John F. Kennedy's speech writer and executive assistant **Ted Sorenson**, debated in high school and college.

• **Oprah Winfrey** competed in debate in high school.

• **Tom Brokaw** debated at South Dakota State.

• In his book, *Confessions*, **St. Augustine** writes, "from age 18 to 35, I was a teacher of public speaking."

- In addition to the many celebrated debates of his public career, **Malcolm X** debated teams from Harvard, Yale, and other New England colleges as part of the Norfolk Prison (Massachusetts) debating program. Read more about it in "*'I Was Gone on Debating'*: *Malcolm X's Prison Debates and Public Confrontations*", by Robert Branham, debate coach at Bates College, published in **Argumentation and Advocacy**, v. 31, Winter, 1995.

- **Cicero, Demosthenes, Plato, Socrates, and Aristotle.**

Cicero's *"De Oratore"*, now at the **British Museum**.

Oratory is attractive but difficult http://bit.ly/1eAC7FF

Cicero claims that in Athens, "where the supreme power of oratory was both invented and perfected," no other art study has a more vigorous life than the art of speaking.

After first trying rhetoric without training or rules, using only natural skill, young orators listened and learned from Greek orators and teachers, and soon were much more enthusiastic for eloquence.

Young orators learned, through practice, the importance of variety and frequency of speech. In the end, orators were awarded with popularity, wealth, and reputation.

But Cicero warns that oratory fits into more arts and areas of study than people might think. This is the reason why this particular subject is such a difficult one to pursue. Students of oratory must have a knowledge of many matters to have successful rhetoric. They must also form a certain style through word choice and arrangement. Students must also learn to understand human emotion so as to appeal to their audience.

This means that the student must, through his style, bring in humor and charm—as well as the readiness to deliver and respond to an attack.

Moreover, a student must have a significant capacity for memory—they must remember complete histories of the past, as well as of the law.

Cicero reminds us of another difficult skill required for a good orator: a speaker must deliver with control—using gestures, playing and expressing with features, and changing the intonation of the voice.

In summary, oratory is a combination of many things, and to succeed in maintaining all of these qualities is a great achievement.

Amazon reviewer George R. Dekle: http://amzn.to/18xOpwX

"This is a review of "De Oratore" books I-II and "De Oratore" book III in the Loeb Classical Library. Marcus Tullius Cicero wrote much on many subjects, and some of his private correspondence also survives. He did his best writing in the field of rhetoric. Although he was not an original thinker on the subject of rhetoric, "De Oratore" shows him to have had an encyclopedic practical knowledge of oratory in general and criminal trial advocacy in particular.

Cicero wrote "De Oratore" as a dialog among some of the preeminent orators of the era immediately preceding Cicero's time. The occasion is a holiday at a country villa, and the characters discuss all facets of oratory, ceremonial, judicial, and deliberative. They devote most of the discussion to judicial oratory, and their discussion reveals the trial of a Roman lawsuit to be somewhat analogous to the trial of a modern lawsuit. You have to piece it together from stray references to procedure scattered throughout the work, but it appears that a Roman trial consisted of opening statements, the taking of evidence, and final arguments. Modern trial advocacy manuals devote most of their attention to the taking of evidence, but Cicero dismisses the mechanics of presenting evidence as relatively unimportant compared to the mechanics of presenting argument.

"De Oratore" is divided into three books. The first speaks of the qualities of the orator; the second of judicial oratory, and the third of ceremonial and deliberative oratory. The modern trial lawyer would find the second book most interesting and most enlightening. A lot about trial advocacy has changed since Cicero's day (e.g. no more testimony taken under torture), but a lot hasn't.

Trial lawyers cannot congregate without swapping "war stories," and Cicero's characters are no exception. They pepper their discussion with references to courtroom incidents which have such verisimilitude that they could have happened last week instead of 2,000 years ago. I have no doubt that Cicero, had he lived today, would have made a formidable trial lawyer."

Are there any drawbacks to debating?

Yes! There can be arguments, shouting, insults, even physical attacks if a debate is not conducted in a respectful manner. It is therefore essential to ensure that debaters are taught to "disagree agreeably". Dr. Snider lists an excellent, "Code of the Debater" (Snider, 1999, p.13) in his book. Three rules of his Code of Conduct were taught:

1. I will respect the rights of others to freedom of speech.

2. I will respect my partners, opponents, judges and coaches.

3. I will be a generous winner and a gracious loser.

How was debating taught to sixth-grade students?

First, the class was informed that for the final three weeks they would be debating. The students were then divided into six mixed-ability teams of four students each. One of the best students was selected to be my "Assistant Coach".

Next, the meanings of the terms: *resolution, affirmative team*, and *negative team* were explained. Turn-taking was explained: One member of the affirmative team speaks first, then one from the negative team. This continues until everyone has spoken.

After that, the speaking roles of the four team members were explained. The first speaker on each team is the Captain. This person introduces their teammates and outlines the main arguments their team will make. The second and third speaker for each team, in turn, presents their argument for, or against, the resolution.

The final speaker for each team summarises the arguments their team has made. It must be noted that each speaker briefly *refutes* (finds fault with) the previous speaker's arguments. Additionally, one question from the opposing team had to be answered by the second and third speaker on each team.

The "winner" is the team that has scored highest in three categories: **teamwork** (strategy), **content** (argument) and **delivery** (how well the speech was made). The students are judged on a scale of 1 – 10 in each category with 30 points being a perfect score.

The judge's decision is final. After announcing the winner, the judge briefly explains the debate scoring and offers constructive criticism to both teams. Respectful discussion, including questions and opinions, are allowed by both teams.

This kind of immediate, two-way, post-debate feedback is essential because it helps students to improve their performance as debaters.

As a fun, motivational activity, the class copied and memorized the following, "Debater's Creed" from the movie, "The Great Debaters":

Denzel: "Who is the judge?"

Debaters: "God is the judge."

Denzel: "Why is God the judge?"

Debaters: "Because God decides who's right or wrong, not my opponent."

Denzel: "Who's your opponent?"

Debaters: "My opponent doesn't exist."

Denzel: "Why does your opponent not exist?"

Debaters: "Because our opponent is a voice dissenting from the truth I speak."

Denzel: "Speak the truth."

Debaters: "Speak the truth."

Final preparation

In the next class the students reviewed what they had learned in the previous class. After that, each team captain introduced his teammates. Next, each team said the Debater's Creed. This was done in order; one team after the other rather than as a class. The Assistant Coach circulated from team to team and prompted students who needed help.

After that, all teams were given the same debate resolution: Resolved – "Spiderman is better than Superman". Working together, each team now had to decide what their arguments were going to be and in what order they would speak. The author and the Assistant Coach circulated, helping with vocabulary and grammar. At the end of the class the debate pairings/matches were agreed upon for the next class.

The debates

It was decided that all speeches would last one minute. The Assistant Coach was the timekeeper. This author was both the Debate Chairperson and Judge. Each team debated on a resolution twice; once as the affirmative team and once as the negative team. After that the resolution was changed. While two teams were debating, the other four teams were the audience. The students debated the following resolutions:

Spiderman is better than Superman.
School uniforms are not necessary.
School should last year-round with no summer holiday.
Students should not have to take tests.
Fast food restaurants should be banned.

CONCLUSION

To sum up, the debates were lively and fun with all students participating. Debating was easily taught and quickly learned. Students used grammar and vocabulary they had learned during the year. This recycling helped them revise and consolidate their previous learning. They worked collaboratively and got practice in public speaking. Critical thinking skills were used to develop and refute arguments. Debating proved to be an enjoyable way to productively finish the year for the students. Finally, I recommend debating for all teachers, since it can be easily adapted to almost any teaching context.

WORKS CITED

Baker, T. J. (2012): Teaching Debate in Chile. Lexington, Ky: CreateSpace Publishing House. http://bit.ly/159qVvp

Manning, M. & Nakamura, T. (2006). Teaching Debate in the EFL Classroom.

Snider, A. (1999). The code of the debater: Introduction to the way of reason. USA. Sponsored by the Open Society Institute, the World Debate Institute and the University of Vermont.

Tomasello, M. (2003). The key is social cognition. In *Language in mind; advances in the study of language and thought*. ed. D. Gentner and S. Goldin-Meadow.

Tomasello, M., Kruger, A. C., and Ratner, H. H. (1993). Cultural learning. *Behavioral and Brain Sciences*, 16, 495–552.

Vygotsky, L. (1962). Thought and language. Cambridge, MA: MIT Press. (Original work published 1934.)

_____ (1978). Mind in society: The development of higher psychological processes. ed. M. Cole. Cambridge, MA: Harvard University Press.

Washington, Denzel. (2007). The Great Debaters. Harpo Films.

CHAPTER 2

WHAT DOES A DEBATE COACH DO?

"Learning to debate means learning how to think." ~ Unknown

You just found out you're going to coach your school debate team. You're thrilled, right? Well, if you're like most debate coaches I have met, you got the job by being told you were going to be the debate coach. Non-negotiable. Sound familiar, huh?

OK, you're the coach of the debate team. You can't get out of it, so now what? Well, first of all, you need a team. You have to recruit some debaters.

What? How did I recruit debaters? In my case, I promised them an extra week of winter vacation. No, not really, I'm just kidding.

Here's some ideas, taken from an imaginative dialog:

Me: Remember what happened to you? You were told that you were the coach. So tell the students they are on your team.

You: What? That won't work!

Me: Hmm. Worked fine for me. But maybe that won't work for you. Alright, beg.

You: Beg?

Me: Beg. I'm serious. Beg the students to come to a tryout.

How to Coach a Debate Team

You: What? That won't work either. Nobody will come!

Me: I understand your dilemma. Hmm, how about this: **Be Honest**. Tell the students that debating requires long hours of practice. Tell them there is lots of research they have to do. Tell them debating is difficult, and all you can guarantee them is lots of long hours perfecting their debating skills.

You: What? Are you serious?

Me: Yes.

You: Do I have any other options?

Me: How about a movie? The most inspiring debating movie I can suggest is *"The Great Debaters"*, starring Denzell Washington. After they watch that movie, they will want to go out and debate somebody, anybody. Trust me, it is truly amaaaaaaaazing!

To sum up, your first step in being a debate coach is to recruit a team. As a matter of fact, it's the most important thing you do. Recruit a team. Any way that you can, recruit a team.

Why?

Because a debate coach without a team is not a debate coach.

What if you have a team, now what? Watch these videos: http://bit.ly/Kja3rO

Debate Delivers Dreams:
http://bit.ly/MJkSqd

**

More Reasons Why Teaching Debate is A Very Good Idea

Thomas Jerome Baker

Teaching debate, in Chile, or anywhere else in the world, is clearly a worthwhile endeavour. The purpose of this additional bit of encouragement for the debate coach is to share with you, the reader, my absolute certainty about the value of debate. I will give only three reasons, as I value your time. However, it must be said that there are many more than three (3) reasons why teaching debate is a good idea.

Firstly, the skills of debate will help you to solve disagreements peacefully. Thus, conflict is avoided. By conflict, I mean outright violence, whether physical or verbal. For example, let me mention the Arab-Israeli conflict. On an almost daily basis, the world news reports of some new fighting, some new bloodshed, some new atrocity.

Debating, in my view, is a more peaceful alternative. In a civilized world, regardless of all evidence to the contrary, it is possible to resolve disagreements through peaceful means. Even if the only thing you can do, is agree to disagree, debating is more productive (and life-preserving) than aggression.

Secondly, I want to emphasize that debating develops critical thinking. It teaches participants how to think for themselves. In a debate, for instance, you must listen carefully to the assertions of the opposite team. Any unsupported information that is relevant to the debate will be challenged.

You ask, for example, "Who is your expert opinion from? What is the source of your information?" You do this so often, time and again, that it becomes a natural habit of mind. Thus, debating is an excellent way to promote critical thinking. Without this capacity, we could be easily influenced, and in many instances, with undesirable outcomes, even negative personal consequences.

Thirdly, and most importantly, debating is about persuasion. People are persuaded for various reasons. For some, it is logic and rationality. For others, it is cultural, social, or even emotional. This awareness makes you more likely to be objective, rather than subjective, when making important decisions in your life.

How to Coach a Debate Team

Why is this a good idea?

For example, when a politician uses a slogan, such as, "Let's Change the World", you might ask, "What's Your Plan?" Rather than being swayed by the emotional prospect of a changed world, you now ask for substance. In essence, you are more objective, not easily persuaded by hollow phrases designed to appeal to you emotionally.

In conclusion, I have shared what I consider to be three important reasons why learning to debate is a good idea. In my book, "Teaching Debate in Chile, I list more reasons, and take a look at these reasons from various perspectives.

Finally, these three reasons, without the shadow of a doubt, are important for everyone. To put this as sincerely as possible, we all want to live in a better world. To do that, we need to know how to talk to one another when we are in disagreement. Therefore debate is a powerful tool to use. When we debate, peace, critical thinking and objectivity are all promoted. In today's world, and the better world of the future, these three aspects are, and will continue to be, highly desirable.

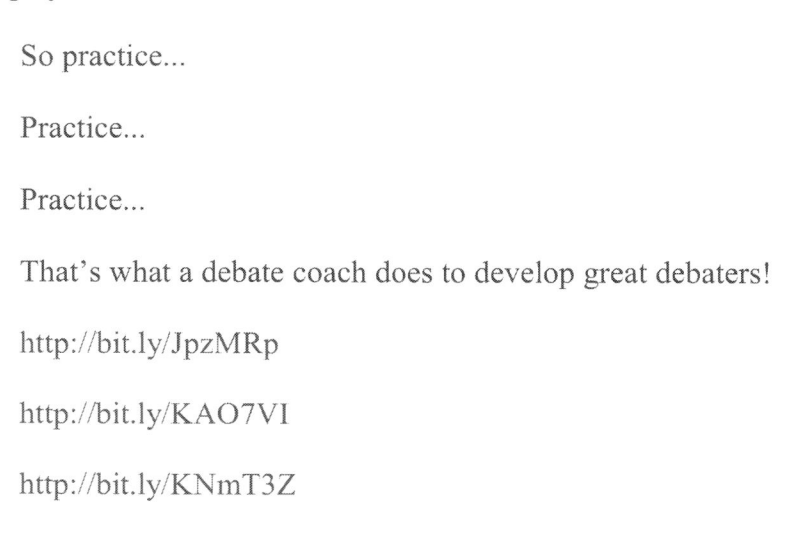

So practice...

Practice...

Practice...

That's what a debate coach does to develop great debaters!

http://bit.ly/JpzMRp

http://bit.ly/KAO7VI

http://bit.ly/KNmT3Z

CHAPTER 3

GENERAL EQUALITY DEBATE

"It is a great point to have the main point in mind." ~

*APEC recognizes that a successful society can result only from the full participation of women in the economy, and has strived to promote **gender equality** through such organizations as the **Women Leaders Network (WLN)** and the **Gender Focal Point Network (GFPN)**. These and other bodies are charged with studying policy and promoting best practices regarding gender equality and making recommendations to APEC Ministers regarding how best to enable full participation of women in the economic and civic life of their societies.

As traditional economies and industries adopt more inclusive practices, it is important to reflect on the fundamental shifts necessary to achieve the successful implementation of gender equality.

In this regard, we must consider the cultural traditions, norms, and practices of the economies in which we conduct business, and the unique capabilities that women bring to the workplace.

Many women around the world are moving into senior management positions within large transnational corporations. For some APEC economies, this change in gender among the upper level staff might cause a bit of discomfort.

This teaching tip will allow students to debate gender issues arising in the current business environment.

How to Coach a Debate Team

Content Objectives

To debate gender discrimination in business

To apply the three rules of conduct for a debate

Language Objectives

To apply the language of agreement and disagreement in a respectful manner

To use the acronym A-R-E-T to plan, present, and justify one's position

Activity

1. Explain three rules for student behavior (Snider, 1999).

    a. I will respect the rights of others to freedom of speech
    b. I will respect my partners, opponents, and judges.
    c. I will be a generous winner and a gracious loser.

2. Explain the acronym A-R-E-T to plan, present, and justify one's position (Baker, 2009):

A: Argument - A woman should receive the same salary as a man for the same job.

R: Reason(s) - A woman does the same quality and quantity of work as a man.

E: Evidence - A business manager, executive, or administrator does the same job, regardless of gender.

T: Therefore - Therefore, a woman ought to receive equal pay for equal work.

3. Explain the four speaking roles for each team:

1st Speaker (Captain) –
Outlines the main arguments the team will make.

2nd Speaker –
Presents the team's arguments for or against the topic.

3rd Speaker –
Presents the team's arguments for or against the topic.

4th Speaker –
Summarizes the team's arguments and closes the debate.

4. Explain the rules for turn-taking and timing:

a. The team in favor of the topic, pro, speaks first.
b. The team against the topic, con, speaks second.
c. Speakers alternate speaking turns until everyone has spoken.
d. All speakers speak for 3 minutes each.

5. The teacher describes and clarifies the chosen debate topic (see list of topics under Materials) and makes teams.

6. Ask which students would like to be pro (in agreement) and con (against).

7. Select four students to speak on each team.

8. Allow the students sufficient time to prepare their arguments together. (Students can use their notes but should not read their presentations word-for-word).

9. The two teams sit in front of the class to debate.

10. When they finish, the class members in the audience can question people on either team.

11. After the question and answer period, the audience votes on which team was the most convincing.

Materials

List of possible debate topics to choose from:

1. Women should receive the same salary as men for the same job.

2. Mothers who work outside the home neglect their children.

3. A woman should not receive a position that makes her the boss if the culture makes it difficult for a man to accept being subordinate to a woman.

4. If the number of female executives in a company is low, a woman should be promoted, even if the best applicant is a man.

5. Hiring a woman is a nightmare because of maternity leave and fears of sexual discrimination lawsuits. Equality laws, therefore, actually hold women in business back from economic opportunity.

Category
Women in Business: Gender discrimination

Learning Theme
Learning to do; problem solving

*What is APEC?

According to Wikipedia, "Asia-Pacific Economic Cooperation (APEC) is a forum for 21 Pacific Rim countries (formally Member Economies) that seeks to promote free trade and economic cooperation throughout the Asia- Pacific region. Established in 1989 in response to the growing interdependence of Asia-Pacific economies and the advent of regional economic blocs (such as the European Union) in other parts of the world, APEC works to raise living standards and education levels through sustainable economic growth and to foster a sense of community and an appreciation of shared interests among Asia-Pacific countries. Members account for approximately 40% of the world's population, approximately

54% of the world's gross domestic product and about 44% of world trade. An annual APEC Economic Leaders' Meeting is attended by the heads of government of all APEC members except Taiwan (represented under the name Chinese Taipei) by aministerial-level official. The location of the meeting rotates annually among the member economies, and until 2011, a famous tradition involved the attending leaders dressing in a national costume of the host member.

What kind of work does the Women Leaders Network (WLN) and the Gender Focal Point Network (GFPN) do?

These and other bodies are charged with studying policy and promoting best practices regarding gender equality and making recommendations to APEC Ministers regarding how best to enable full participation of women in the economic and civic life of their societies. As traditional economies and industries adopt more inclusive practices, it is important to reflect on the fundamental shifts necessary to achieve the successful implementation of gender equality. In this regard, we must consider the cultural traditions, norms, and practices of the economies in which we conduct business, and the unique capabilities that women bring to the workplace.

Many women around the world are moving into senior management positions within large transnational corporations. For some APEC economies, this change in gender among the upper level staff might cause a bit of discomfort. This teaching tip will allow students to debate gender issues arising in the current business environment.

Resources
Baker, T. (2009). Debating in the EFL classroom. *International House Journal of Education and Development*, 27. **Retrieved from ihjournal.com/debating-in-the-efl-classroom**

Snider, A. (2008). *The code of the debater: Introduction to policy debating*. New York: International Debate Education Association.

CHAPTER 4

DEBATERS, DEFINITIONS FIRST!

DEBATE, ARGUMENT, DIALOGUE, RHETORIC?

When two people, or two teams begin to debate something, an impartial observer often notices that the debate seems to be about two different things. The debaters energetically take their positions, delivering points and counterpoints. The clue to this divergence that we observe is that the teams have different understandings / interpretations of what they are debating.

Consequently, when the debate finishes, both teams legitimately feel like winners. After all, the other team failed to refute your argument. They never engaged with you because they had nothing to say, right?

Your rhetoric was robust, your arguments were awesome, your dialogue was delivered as both prologue and epilogue. You are clear that your team should definitely win the debate. You have left no doubt in anyone's mind... (Again, both teams feel this way)

To avoid this disappointment and the frustration it brings (for the teams, the adjudicators and the audience) debaters are required to not only define their terms, i.e. what the debate is about, but also to reach an agreement about what the key terms in the resolution (debate topic) mean when they use the key terms in the debate.

To not do this is called a, "**squirrel**", and it is frowned upon.

Squirrels basically want to "get the nut" for themselves, and a debater who "squirrels" or practices squirreling, is trying to make it impossible for the other team to have a fair chance to win.

Debates are supposed to be 50 – 50 propositions, not clear-cut, and therefore, the possibility of winning, or losing, is equal for both sides.

To win, you have to engage with the other side's arguments, clearly show those arguments are not true, not important, or will result in some undesirable negative consequences. On the other hand, your team's arguments are bigger, better, more important, and will result in some desirable consequence that outweighs any negatives that may be associated with it.

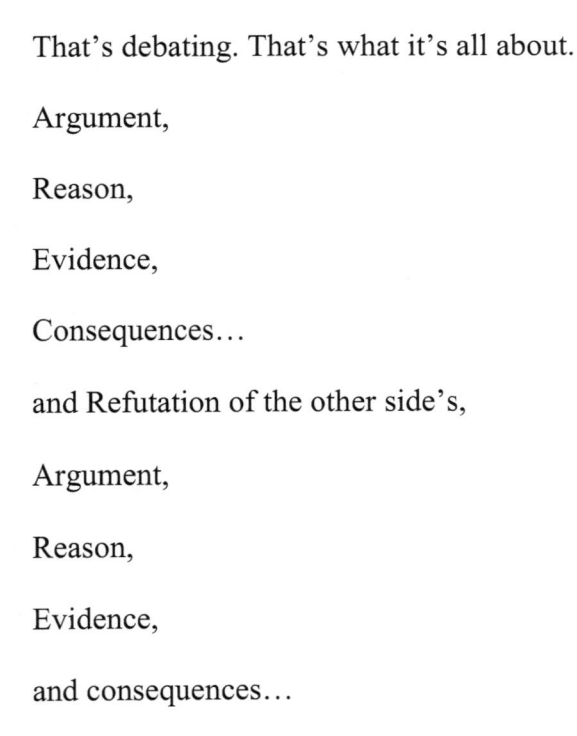

That's debating. That's what it's all about.

Argument,

Reason,

Evidence,

Consequences…

and Refutation of the other side's,

Argument,

Reason,

Evidence,

and consequences…

To do it right, to debate in this fashion, you have got to define your terms, or otherwise it gets to be quite ugly, with both sides having a one-way argument with…themselves.

Defining terms and reaching agreements about how those terms are being used is an imperative for a beautiful debate to take place...

http://bit.ly/KcAPTK

**

THE FINAL DEBATE SPEECH: HOW TO DELIVER THE CLOSING ARGUMENT

The debate is almost over. You've got one more speech to make, the final one. What do you do?

What do you say? How do you say it? Does it even matter?

Let's face it, if you haven't been convincing by now, it's too late. Judges are humans. They make decisions based on first impressions, rarely on last impressions.

That's just the way humans are – we're "wired" that way. Where does it come from, this "make up your mind early" way of making decisions.

Answer: I don't know. But here's an experiment: Ask anybody, male or female – if they would consider dating someone who made a bad first impression. My guess is that 75% (for No) is a conservative estimate.

I have one more experiment for you. Ask anyone who has to interview people for a job, for employment. Ask that person if they would consider giving anyone a second interview – if they had a bad first impression. My guess is that 90% (again, No) is a conservative estimate.

What's my point? I'm simply trying to say if you have 2 speakers – a "weak" speaker and a "strong" speaker, then where you put the speakers matter.

If you're like most debate coaches, your weak speaker is first and your strong speaker is last.

Right?

It's human nature to "save the best for last". Well, in debating, don't do that. Do the opposite. Why?

Debating is a verbal sport, and as such, you want to "verbally hit" your opponent hard and often – before they hit you back.

Think of it like being in a physical battle.

Unless you are Muhammad Ali, do you really want to be "hit" by George Foreman, hard and often, until George gets tired, before you "hit" George?

Not me.

I put a sledgehammer in my gloves and go to pounding on George, hard and often, before he hits me. Many people speculate that Muhammad Ali suffered Parkinsons as a cumulative result of being hit, hard and often, by George Foreman and Joe Frazier.

What can we learn from this?

Don't let heavyweight punchers hit you – it's bad for your health. Seriously, I'm not kidding. Don't let other people "hit on you", neither in a boxing match, nor in a debating match. Defend yourself when you must, "hit your opponent" as hard as you can, whenever you can, as soon as you can, as often as you can. "Take the fight to the other team". Use your offense as your best defensive strategy.

Enough boxing metaphors. Let me be clear now.

In the evolution of the human race, species, early Cave Men had to make a split second "Friend or Foe", "Fight or Flight" decision every time they met a new person. This was our survival instinct.

Well, we as a species, the human race has evolved, but the survival instinct is still intact.

We still have those survival tendencies. Quickly size up a person, decide whether or not someone is trustworthy, and quickly move on to other business.

Well, judges are humans. Don't make them wait until the end of a debate to find out you have a strong debater on your team. Let that strong debater speak first, and have the other debaters build on what was accomplished – through the use of the team line and the team split – and your final speaker – the "weak speaker" will have a wonderful time closing out the debate for your team.

On those rare occasions when the debate is evenly matched, a cohesive strategy – from beginning to end – keeping your arguments unified while constantly showing your arguments are bigger, more important, more relevant, cheaper, causing few drawbacks while achieving the greater good, the most benefits – then you will be in a positive position for the final speech, a winning speech.

Finally, what does a winning final speech look like, sound like, feel like? How do you stand and deliver this important speech?

Let me give you a scenario here:

You want to be the Prime Minister of Canada. OK? Prime Minister of Canada. Can you close your eyes and imagine that?

Great.

Next, the debate is now down to the final speech.

What would you say to the people of Canada?

Why should Canadians trust you? Is there anyone who they should distrust? What are you going to do that somebody else is not going to do?

Honestly, I don't have a clue. But take a moment to try to answer the questions. Then watch the video that follows. Listen to *what* they say. Listen to *how* they say *what* they say.

Next, turn the sound off. *Watch the body language.* Who is looking at you? Who is moving their hands in a natural manner? Who is reading a prepared speech to you?

Now, who do you trust? Who seems to have more **credibility**, more trustworthiness? Why?

Well, now you know. Now you know how to deliver a final speech, a closing argument. Now you can argue, without arguing...

Oh, I almost forgot. Here is the video. Just go to the website where the link takes you to. http://bit.ly/KcBncu

One more thing. Passively watching a video is a good way of learning, especially if you have chosen your video resource material wisely. Nonetheless, it goes without saying that simply watching someone else make an important speech is not going to be enough for you to be able to do the same.

You have got to put into practice the lessons you have learned through observation. Through diligent application of the principles and fundamentals of delivering an effective speech, you will increase your skill at this element of debating, namely, making the closing argument.

I have turned to the past to find a great speech, a conclusion to an important persuasive speech. The speech was made over 100 years ago by Daniel Webster, and has been all but forgotten. It suits our purposes well because it is the kind of speech that students can use to practice their ability to stand and deliver the closing argument.

It is the conclusion of Webster's speech, delivered in the United States Senate, on, *"The Presidential Veto of the United States Bank Bill"*. Notice the skillful interweaving of conviction and persuasion, and remember that this is the conclusion of a speech containing about 14,000 words. The speech to practice, reading aloud (not to be memorised), is as follows:

"Mr. President, we have arrived at a new epoch. We are entering on experiments, with the government and the Constitution of the country, hitherto untried, and of fearful and appalling aspect. This message calls us to the contemplation of a future which little resembles the past.

Its principles are at war with all that public opinion has sustained, and all which the experience of the government has sanctioned. It denies first principles; it contradicts truths, hitherto received as indisputable.

It denies to the judiciary the interpretation of law, and claims to divide with Congress the power of originating statutes. It extends the grasp of executive pretension over every power of the government. But this is not all.

It presents the chief magistrate of the Union in the attitude of arguing away the powers of that government over which he has been chosen to preside; and adopting for this purpose modes of reasoning which, even under the influence of all proper feeling towards high official station, it is difficult to regard as respectable.

It appeals to every prejudice which may betray men into a mistaken view of their own interests, and to every passion which may lead them to disobey the impulses of their understanding. It urges all the specious topics of State rights and national encroachment against that which a great majority of the States have affirmed to be rightful, and in which all of them have acquiesced.

It sows, in an unsparing manner, the seeds of jealousy and ill-will against that government of which its author is the official head. It raises a cry, that liberty is in danger, at the very moment when it puts forth claims to powers heretofore unknown and unheard of.

It affects alarm for the public freedom, when nothing endangers that freedom so much as its own unparalleled pretences. This, even, is not all.

It manifestly seeks to inflame the poor against the rich; it wantonly attacks whole classes of the people, for the purpose of turning against them the prejudices and the resentment of other classes.

It is a state paper which finds no topic too exciting for its use, no passion to inflammable for its address and its solicitation.

Such is this message. It remains now for the people of the United States to choose between the principles here avowed and their government.

These cannot subsist together.

The one or the other must be rejected.

If the sentiments of the message shall receive general approbation, the Constitution will have perished even earlier than the moment which its enemies originally allowed for the termination of its existence. It will not have survived to its fiftieth year." [Source: Webster's Great Speeches, page 338.]

**

There is little doubt that your students will have great fun delivering this speech. Not only that, because it contains masterful use of persuasive rhetoric to be used in the delivery of an effective conclusion. In other words, here is a speech worth studying to understand its powers of persuasion, on the one hand, and to interpret it through speech, on the other...

CHAPTER 5

THE RIGHT TO DIE

Debating in Chile's Public Schools

No, this is not an oxymoron. The terms, "debate" and "Chile" and "public school" are not mutually exclusive. There are some very good, sometimes even, great debates in Chile, in the public school sector. Firstly, here's a fundamental question:

Why is debating a good idea?

There are a thousand answers to that question, and all of them are good. However, here's the answer that I like best:

"Why should we teach our students to debate, you ask? After all, debating is competitive, there's a winner and a loser. Shouldn't teachers be teaching their students how to cooperate, rather than compete?

Here's a global answer to the question(s):

"Sooner or later, all the people of the world will have to discover a way to live together in peace... If this is to be achieved, man must evolve for all human conflict a method which rejects revenge, aggression, and retaliation..." ~ Dr. Martin Luther King, Jr. - 1964 Nobel Peace Prize Acceptance Speech

I'm sure you will agree that Dr. King's answer is both eloquent and powerful. So, we *are* convinced. Now, what about the debate in Chile?

This competition, organized by the English Opens Doors Program (Inglés Abre Puertas Program (PIAP), is aimed at students of Secondary Schools and the government funded municipal schools. The issue which was debated at this opportunity:

"This House Believes That (THBT) the right to die is the ultimate personal freedom".

Each team researches and prepares to debate, both in favor as well as against, before sorting the position they will have to defend. Here's the basic principle which serves as the foundation for this debate:

"All humans have rights, especially the right to dignity."

Universally, almost all people would quickly agree that human dignity is a basic human right that must be respected at all times.

But what happens when respecting someone's dignity – prevents you from saving someone's life?

That's what this debate is all about, namely: Do I have the right to take my own life, in a dignified manner, when I reach the conclusion that my life is no longer worth living because of some problem that is negatively affecting the quality of my life?

Do I have the right to die – as the ultimate expression of personal freeedom???

A simple toss of the coin decides whether your team is pro (in favor) or contra (against).

How will the debates turn out?

I do not know. Winning a debate involves many aspects, so it's less important to focus on winning or losing. If you focus on how each member of the team makes an individual contribution to the success of the team, the results will always be favorable – win or lose.

Why do I say that?

Because debating is more about the skills you must develop in order to participate. A student must learn to research effectively, practice giving speeches, and be a good listener. These are skills that serve people throughout their entire lives, and that fact alone makes debating an outstanding activity, recommendable for all students.

Again, in debating, you enjoy the journey. It's not about winning, it's about participating. In the end, you discover that everyone's a winner...

http://bit.ly/KcBncu

Stonehenge at midnight

CHAPTER 6

DEATH PENALTY DEBATE

Debate Coach, you have just received the motion for your next debate. Your team needs to begin the process of preparing arguments for, and against, the motion. Here's the motion:

"This House Believes That (THBT) the death penalty should be abolished."

Well, the first thing you should do is hope that your team ends up debating the affirmative. This is a topic that lends itself well to the proposition team. Why? Quite frankly, no society on Earth condones the killing of human beings. We allow only three "exceptions": war, self-defense, and legal punishment. This third exception, legal punishment (a death sentence) is an exception that many feel should be eliminated.

Coach, if you are unlucky, your team must argue the negative. How can you possibly hope to win a debate in which you know the other team will be eloquent, well-researched, and genuinely PASSIONATE, emotionally involved, with their hearts, souls, and minds?

Let's be honest. You know you can't win, and your debaters know they can't win. So, you show up for the debate, make your speeches, and accept your loss. Right?

Wrong.

Firstly, debating isn't about winning or losing. If that's the approach you have been using, then it's time to stop. Now. Debating isn't, not now, nor has it ever been, a zero-sum game.

The motto, "if I win, you lose" is out of place in debating. Debating is about teaching young people to be critical thinkers, to see both sides of an issue, to express themselves clearly and articulately, and to make the world a better place for everyone to live in. Agreed?

So, let's go back to the Death Penalty debate. Review with your team the basics of debating: Ethos, Pathos, Logos. Your team will need to use all three in this debate, but especially "Logos" (logic).

The major strength of the affirmative team will be it's Pathos, (emotional appeal) to the judges and audience. As they point out the statistics, the case examples, and the inhumanity of one man killing another, everyone in the room will be mentally associating your team with the Death Penalty. So, what can you do?

Answer: Turn the tables.

Use "Ethos" (personal credibility) to rid yourself of the negative association being attributed to your team. Your team is only debating, they haven't put anyone to death, they haven't killed anyone, and have no plans to do so.

They go to church and believe in the Ten Commandments. Especially the one that says:

"Thou shalt not kill."

(Pause when you say that, while quickly scanning the room, looking everyone in the eye – a millisecond is enough)

In fact, we, and everyone in the room (said looking at the audience – using a broad, wide encircling, inclusive gesture that terminates with the speaker touching their heart – earnest look on face) we all, everyone in this room, we all believe killing is not right.

"Let's be clear, this is only a debate"...

(End of speech)

Coach, your team is now able to go forward with your "Logos", your logic. You begin to go to your statistics, your facts, your figures, all the while making it clear that you live in a society in which everyone believes that no man should kill another man. (You already got the judges, the audience, and even the other team to accept this).

Well, it is not enough to believe this. You must make the choice about how this belief is best protected, and best achieved. That entails making a difficult decision.

That is where we "clash" today. The proposition believes that *even if* one man kills another man, a killer has the right to expect that no man will kill the killer.

The proposition is asking the judges, the audience, to accept that the killer has a right to the protection of a society that believes no man should kill another man.

We clash today because we believe that a killer did not believe in, and did not practice the right to life. The action of the killer clearly shows they do not believe what you and I believe. You and I believe that the right to life is sacred. We believe the right to life is universal. A murderer does not believe in these things.

Therefore, the opposition believes that a killer has forfeited the right to life, and that the biblical doctrine of, "an eye for an eye" should be applied. In fact, to be consistent with our civilized society, based on the fundamental belief in the right to life, the death penalty must be applicable. (*This is your argument*)

In other words, the death penalty is justified as the only penalty possible for anyone who kills another human being. A society who believes life is precious, a society who believes life is sacred, a society who believes no man should kill another man, then *such* a society must accept the unavoidable ultimate consequence of its belief, the death penalty for murderers. Thank you. (*end of speech*)

How to Coach a Debate Team

Debate Coach, now your team has made the debate an even debate. The proposition has *Pathos*, or emotion, on their side. Your team has used *Ethos* (we are not killers) and *Logos* (Logic: society is responsible to hold all life **sacred**, not permit killers to **desecrate** the **sanctity of human life** without paying an equal price-their own life) to counteract their advantage.

From here on out, this would be a great debate. Remember, it's not a zero-sum game. It's not about winning, it's about developing the ability to critically examine an issue, and then reach your own conclusions.

Finally, I've got a great link with some great information about the death penalty. Yes, you must do your research, so the link is **only a starting point.**

Don't forget human, eye to eye, face to face research. Get your team out there talking to victims of crimes, talking to their neighbors, talking to lawyers, judges, doctors, priests and pastors.

Debating, in the end, always comes down to how real people are affected by the issues of the day. You have got to go talk to them, if you wish to speak for them. Oh, here's the link:

Death penalty statistics from the US: which state executes the most people? http://bit.ly/rixBjm

Barack Obama on the Death Penalty: http://bit.ly/Jpxm5k

Question:

If your wife, your husband, or your child child was raped and murdered, would you be in favor of the death penalty?

Click this link for the surprising answer... **http://bit.ly/Ksah0v**

**

CHAPTER 7

PRO OR CONTRA

"We are what we repeatedly do. Excellence then, is not an act, but a habit." ~ Aristotle

In my first debate book, "Teaching Debate in Chile" I covered the basics of debate. With it, a debate coach could more than adequately prepare their team for a debate. What is missing from the book however, is advanced coverage of common debate topics. The purpose of this chapter, and indeed this book, is to address the common debate topics that are often used. In this way, a debate team can reduce significantly the amount of time needed to prepare for a debate.

What that means is that more time can be spent preparing the team for the delivery of the speeches. As you will remember from the previous book, debates are judged on three things:

- **content,**

- **style,** and

- **strategy**.

Using this book wisely will give you more time to work on **style** (speech delivery), while allowing you to quickly decide on matters of **content** and **strategy**.

How does this work? First, there is a poll / survey for you to do. This is your data collection. It provides the debaters with statistics, facts and figures taken randomly, from everyday people who you meet on the street.

On the street?

Yes, on the street. You are talking to real people, face to face. It is important to find out information from real people about how they feel, what their their opinions are, how they are affected, and their genuine reactions to the issues of the day. So, yes, get out on the street and talk to people. Real people. For example:

You: Hi. I'm doing a survey / taking a poll about _____ . Would you mind taking a minute to answer some questions for me?"

Real Person: No problem...

**

Again, as I mentioned above, go on the street, ask for help, and you will be surprised how many people really stop to help you. Remember, this empirical evidence can be used effectively in the preparation and delivery of your debate speeches.

Second, there are four short videos which will examine both sides of the debate topic. This may be done in any manner that presents the issue so that the fundamental principles at stake are clear and understandable.

Thus, insights into how a team might approach the delivery of an effective speech can be gained through careful observation.

That's all there is to it. Ready to give it a go? Let's begin. Good luck in your debate!

"Justice is blind"

DEBATE 1:

MOTION:

THIS HOUSE BELIEVES THAT THE DEATH PENALTY SHOULD NOT BE USED UNDER ANY CIRCUMSTANCES

Let's go to our poll / survey for research data. What do the people say?

How many people agree? What percent?

How many people disagree? What percent?

What percent give an alternate answer?

Are there any interesting comments?

Examine the survey data looking for trends that might support your position.

How to Coach a Debate Team

Next, it's time for both teams to go through six **(6) fundamental steps** to *build their case.*

"What makes a decent World School Debating Championships (WSDC) case?" (Excerpt)

19 november 2008
Poslal Andrej Schulcz
http://bit.ly/p8uplq

An article on what to think of during case building.

The World Schools Debating Championship uses a format that has become as open as never before. There is no single debate strategy that beats all different ones. Nonetheless, the format has also developed a tradition, which now most judges at Worlds expect the teams to follow. This tradition is not unjustified.

On the contrary, it is a tradition of best practice what to look for in case construction before a debate and presenting the case in the twelve or so minutes in the first and second speeches.

This article will attempt to sum up what is expected of debate cases at Worlds, so that debaters will no longer be surprised by the elegance of how other teams state their arguments. In short, what makes a decent WSDC case?

MOTION:

The death penalty should not be used under any circumstances.

Yes or No

Do you agree? Do you disagree?

Consider this possible exception to include in your case:

"Death penalty possible if victim's family asks for capital punishment. Since they have suffered the loss of a family member, directly, the family should have the option to demand capital punishment."

Yes or No

Do you agree? Do you disagree?

Basically, this is a **checklist** of what you should look for in preparation, and what should be included in the first speech of your team, especially if you are in the **proposition**.

While the international rules require only some of the listed items to be included, and they state no order in which they should be presented, all of them should be dealt with in one way or the other, and for less experienced debaters it is better to mention them explicitly, **rather than leave too much to the judge's imagination**.

1. **Introducing the debate**

Funny or serious, examples or generalizations, this is a moment for style. No natter what your style is, make it clear to the judges why the debate topic is important. Be clear about why it matters, and to whom.

2. **Defining what the debate should be about**

Define the key terms of the debate. Be explicit. Use an authoritative dictionary, current year edition. Alternatively, set the parameters, or borders, of the debate. This lets the judges and the opposing team know what you define as being outside the limits of the debate topic.

3. **Specifying the team's position**

Now it's time to clearly state your position you will stand for, or against. This plan is called a "**model**" and can accept all, or parts of the debate motion. In our death penalty debate, for example, you can accept that it is 100% eliminated, no death penalty in no circumstance, or you could name exceptions in which you would apply the death penalty (war crimes, mass murderers, child murderers, when police are killed, etc.)

The opposing side can also do the same, in effect making a counter-proposal, instead of simply opposing the death penalty. In such a case, the opposing team is conceding the point, (no death penalty) but attempting to prove they have a better plan, or model, that is bigger, better, cheaper, or more beneficial than what the other team is proposing to do.

Note, this is the format of the World Schools Debating Championships (WSDC), an international competition. You will have to check your local rules to see if any restrictions apply on your local, regional, or national level. In sum, the judges, and the opposing team expect to be clearly told what your plan (model) is. This is absolutely necessary.

4. **Presenting the team line**

This is a sentence, or line, that everyone on the team will say.

This is the 'big picture' to your case." Work on your individual arguments first, and the big idea, will emerge naturally. This team line unites all the speeches, and is strategically important.

For instance, in the motion, "This House Believes That the death penalty should not be used under any circumstances", the proposition could say: "We will uphold the right to life and avoid irrevocable errors, – You can't say, "Sorry" to a dead man who was innocent!

The opposition would state their team line explicitly, saying perhaps, "The decision is difficult, but the death penalty is the only adequate solution for a society that values the lives of its members!

5. **Splitting the case**

This is simply, *who* speaks, on *what* topics.

To illustrate, in this death penalty debate, the first speaker of the proposition may not want to simply say that their team will have an **economic** and a **moral argument**, and one about the **quality** of life improsonment, but be a bit more creative.

Instead, they could say: "I will look at why our model is needed for **financial reasons**, and why this is the **just model**, and **our second speaker** will talk about **how it will improve the quality** of justice for society in general and the murderer in particular."

6. Presenting the arguments

Finally, you focus on the *persuasive force* of the arguments.

You can do this since you have quickly put your case together, by stating your **definitions,** your **model** and your **case division** (team split) properly. Again, the aim of this Advanced Debating chapter is not to make your arguments for you, but to make your case preparation efficient.

You know what must be done, what is needed, and you do it, leaving your team with ample time to master your arguments. Once you get used to this process of rapid debate preparation, you don't have to focus on what makes a good case, but what makes a good debate – the arguments...

**

Jeremy Irons talks about the death penalty: http://bit.ly/LscXvg

California's Death Penalty: "The death penalty is not about justice, it's about revenge." http://bit.ly/KcHRIg

**

CAPITAL PUNISHMENT (CP) (Practice Debate)

Motion: Capital Punishment should be abolished in the USA.

How to Coach a Debate Team

INTRODUCTION

I. There is at the present time considerable sentiment in the United States in favor of the total abolition of capital punishment.

II. The number of offences punishable by death is continually decreasing.

III. Certain foreign countries, and some of the territories of the United States, have already passed laws prohibiting CP.

IV. The question at issue is: Should this prohibition be extended to every state in the USA?

AFFIRMATIVE TEAM (Abolish Capital Punishment)

I. Capital punishment is unnecessary; for,—

A. Justice may be secured by imprisonment; for,—
1. Society is adequately protected by the incarceration of the offender.

B. Life imprisonment is more feared by criminals than death itself; for,—
1. It often inflicts greater suffering upon the victim.

II. Capital punishment has evil effects upon the community; for,—

A. It diminishes the sacredness in which human life is, held, for,—
1. If the State claims that it is justified in killing those of its citizens who commit given offences, then individuals feel that they are justified for taking life under similar circumstances.

B. It tends to lower the moral sense of the public; for,—
1. Capital punishment is usually accompanied by lots of publicity.
2. Capital punishment methods are cruel (e.g., electrocution).

C. It causes such public sympathy that justice is thwarted; for,—
1. Juries often acquit a man rather than sentence him to death.

III. Capital punishment is unsound sociologically; for,—

A. It does not try to reform the prisoner; for,—
1. Death usually follows closely upon conviction.

B. It arouses the worst passions in men; for,—
1. It is barbaric: "an eye for an eye, and a tooth for a tooth."

IV. Capital punishment is not practical; for,—
A. It has completely failed to stop crime ; for,—
1. Statistics show that where capital punishment is *in force*, crime is on the increase.

V. Reform methods should replace capital punishment; for,—

A. Such methods are sound sociologically.

B. Such methods are more humane.

C. Such methods actually decrease crime.

***

NEGATIVE TEAM (Keep Capital Punishment)

I. Capital punishment is desirable for society; for,—
A. It insures a speedy and effective remedy in those cases where grave crimes are committed against the State.

B. It is the only real preventive of crime; for,—

1. Statistics show that where capital punishment *has been abolished*, crime has greatly increased.

C. It is more economical; for,—

1. It saves the expense of guarding and housing many prisoners.

D. It prevents hardened criminals from being again permitted to committ more crimes.

II. Capital punishment is desirable for criminals themselves; for,—

A. Its severity acts as a deterrent of crime; for,—

1. If a person knows he will be killed if he commits a murder, he is more likely to keep his passions under control than he would be if he would be only imprisoned, with the possibility of pardon later on.

B. It is more humane than life imprisonment; for,—

1. It disposes of the criminal simply and quickly.

III. The objections against capital punishment are not valid; for,—

A. The lives of innocent persons are rarely taken; for,—

1. Courts do not inflict death penalty unless the evidence is conclusive. The death sentence is always reviewed by higher courts.

B. Capital punishment is used only for the most severe crimes; for,—

1. Imprisonment is sufficient for minor crimes.

C. The State must be severe to maintain law and order; for,—

1. A laxity of law enforcement or lenient regulations would result in a great increase in crime; perhaps in anarchy.

2. The State must protect its citizens, no matter how severe a penalty is necessary.

CHAPTER 8

THIS HOUSE BELIEVES SMOKING SHOULD BE PROHIBITED IN ALL PUBLIC PLACES

Time to debate again. You've got a topic:

This house that smoking should be prohibited in all public places.

There are two teams. One is the **affirmative** team. That means you are for the topic. This team must present clear and compelling arguments why smoking should be prohibited in all public places.

The other team is the **negative** team. This team is against the topic. They must present clear and compelling arguments why smoking should NOT be prohibited in all public places.

That isn't all, however. If both teams only present arguments to prove their point of view, then what you have isn't a debate.

It's more like two car salesmen trying to sell you a car. You are going to buy a car. Now, which car is the best car, when both are good?

Well, the salesman who is more persuasive will sell the car to you.

So, what makes this a debate? The same thing that a car salesperson would do if they learned you were considering buying another car. What would they do?

First, they would tell you why the other car, the one you are considering buying, is a bad car. They would convince you the other car is totally wrong for you. They would leave no doubt in your mind that the other car is a bad decision.

Then they would tell you why the car they have is the best car. You'd hear about best price, comfort, speed, status, durability and of course, low gas mileage. Then you would hear about tax benefits. Of course you can have the car in any color you want.

Air conditioning is possible too for the hot summer months. You can also expect low maintenance costs, nothing to worry about. Testimonials from other satisfied car owners would be made available if you want someone to talk to.

To finish, there comes the test drive.

You were born to be wild. Put your shades on. Get your motor running, head out on the highway, wind in your face, your hair flying freely like a rock star, turn up the music, born to be wild, yeaah baby!

Pulling back in the car lot after an exhilirating test drive, you are sold. Time to sign the papers. You just bought yourself a car.

Sorry, I meant a debate. You just won the debate. You have got to destroy the other teams' reasons, and put your own reasons in the best possible light. You do that with clear, convincing, and compelling arguments.

You are like a lawyer, for example, defending a client in a murder trial. Your client is innocent. How is it possible for your client to be in two places at the same time? Innocent is the only verdict possible. No matter what the other lawyer says, to commit the crime, you have to be at the crime scene. Innocent.

Ladies and gentlemen, that is clear and compelling evidence. That's what you do in a debate. You bring the strongest arguments you have. Leave the weak arguments on Google. (really) Oh, and don't forget. Destroy the other team's argument.

Now, you can play it safe and attack all the arguments. But identify the main argument, attack it successfully, and all the other arguments are irrelevant. They don't matter because you proved that your client wasn't at the crime scene.

The gloves, the murder weapon, even the DNA don't matter. How can DNA not matter? How can a murder weapon not matter? How can a bloody pair of shoes not matter?

That's easy. Someone else put them there.

It wasn't your client. Your client wasn't there.

No person can be in two places at the same time.

So what's the verdict? Only one is possible: Innocent.

So dear debaters, never fail to recognize what is the most important thing you have to prove, and then prove it. Otherwise, you will end up with empty hands.

Good luck in your debate, to both teams. By the way, you do know that you have to prepare for both sides of the debate, right? How do you expect to win, if you don't know what the other team is going to say, before they say it?

Prepare for both sides of the debate. It's crucial. Besides, you don't know if you are the affirmative team, or if you will be the negative team. A flip of the coin decides that.

Now, before I close, here are some links to some great resource material:

http://bit.ly/JUa88t   http://bit.ly/qWSjHy

CHAPTER 9

MALCOLM X DEBATES AT OXFORD

"EXTREMISM IN THE DEFENSE OF LIBERTY IS NO VICE"

Malcolm X participated in a classic debate at Oxford Union, a special all university organization as part of Oxford University in England. The debate took place December 3, 1964.

He speaks in favor of the motion that, "extremism in the defense of liberty is no vice".

Do you coach a debate team? Do you use debate with your students, from time to time? Then your students surely have to watch debates on video, right? I know my students watch an incredible number of debates, and a wide variety of speakers and speeches. Why?

Answer: Style. Rhetoric. Delivery. Rhythm. Ethos, Pathos, Logos.

Few speakers in few speeches, few debaters in few debates do what the following speaker did, namely, everything.

If you try to explain it, you will surely attribute it to the urgency of the moment. Immediacy is often the inspiration for extraordinary speeches. This is true for this speech. The speaker was living in a historically urgent time, the African-American struggle for Civil Rights in the USA.

The times were revolutionary ones, transformational ones. The struggle for Civil Rights would leave nobody in the USA indifferent, without an opinion or uncaring of the outcome. It was the time of the great struggle for Civil Rights in the USA, promised a 100 years earlier, in the Emancipation Proclamation, but never a true reality.

Indeed, many would point out that at the time, the state of civil rights in the USA was a direct contradiction of the principle of the right to life, liberty, and the pursuit of happiness enshrined by its Founding Fathers. As Dr. Martin Luther would eloquently put it, I paraphrase: America has issued the Negro a bad check. It has come back from the bank marked, "insufficient funds." America has defaulted on its promise." (see King's, "I Have A Dream" speech).

That is the context of the speech in this debate, the Civil Rights Struggle, definitely an urgent time for any African-American. But it doesn't explain the greatness of Malcolm's speech. Some other quality must be invoked.

I call it **passion**, mixed with **intellect**, mixed with **audacity**, mixed with **eloquence**.

Rhetoric, delivery, presence, rhythm, cadence, logic, intellect, this can be called many things. I would most likely agree with your assessment.

Beyond that, in any case, this is a video that a debater is required to study, for it holds many secrets of persuasive speech…

Enjoy Malcolm X, debating at Oxford University in 1964.

You'll hear X's trademark claim that liberty can be attained by **"whatever means necessary,"** including force, if the government won't guarantee it, and that "intelligently directed extremism" will achieve liberty far more effectively than pacifist strategies. (He's clearly alluding to Martin Luther King.)

I'd also encourage you to watch the dramatic closing minutes and pay some attention to the nice rhetorical slide, where X takes lines from Shakespeare's "Hamlet" and uses them to justify his own position when he uses the phrase, "by whatever means necessary".

You'd probably never expect to see Hamlet getting invoked that way, let alone Malcolm X speaking at Oxford. This is in and of itself a wonderful set of contrasts to be aware of. Let's go to the speech now:

Malcolm X: "I read once, passingly, about a man named Shakespeare. I only read about him passingly, but I remember one thing he wrote that kind of moved me. He put it in the mouth of Hamlet, I think, it was, who said, 'To be or not to be.'

He was in doubt about something—whether it was nobler in the mind of man to suffer the slings and arrows of outrageous fortune—moderation—or to take up arms against a sea of troubles and by opposing end them.

And I go for that. If you take up arms, you'll end it, but if you sit around and wait for the one who's in power to make up his mind that he should end it, you'll be waiting a long time.

And in my opinion, the young generation of whites, blacks, browns, whatever else there is, you're living at a time of extremism, a time of revolution, a time when there's got to be a change.

People in power have misused it, and now there has to be a change and a better world has to be built, and the only way it's going to be built—is with extreme methods.

And I, for one, will join in with anyone—I don't care what color you are—as long as you want to change this miserable condition that exists on this earth." December 3, 1964

Watch the video: http://bit.ly/P6bvx

**

CHAPTER 10

WHAT EVERY DEBATE COACH SHOULD KNOW

(Quote) *"Argumentation is the art of presenting truth so that others will accept it and act in accordance with it."*

~ Goerge K. Pattee, A. M., Assistant Professor of English and Rhetoric, Pennsylvania State College, and author of, *"Practical Argumentation"*, (1909)

Over a hundred years ago, George K. Pattee wrote a book about argumentation that is as good as any other book about debating that you can find today, including the one you are reading now. In his book, Professor Pattee identified and addressed some key elements for debaters.

His table of contents includes the following topics: persuasion, conviction, and speech preparation, among others. This is essential information for any debate coach, in any time period, past, present or future, to know. Accordingly, this book has taken care to adequately address these issues from various perspectives.

It would be well worth our time to allow Professor Pattee to "speak" in his own voice, so that we may take full advantage of a teacher who was interested in the practical side of argumentation, and not merely a theorist. As I have shown throughout this book, it is in the actual practice of debating in which one becomes skilled at debating. So, we are well advised to take a closer look at what he has to say:

Professor George K. Pattee, A. M. (Quoted excerpt, pp. 5-9, 1909) "The practical benefit to be derived from the study and application of the principles of argumentation can hardly be overestimated. The man who wishes to influence the opinions and actions of others, who wishes to become a leader of men in however great or however humble a sphere, must be familiar with this art.

The editor, the lawyer, the merchant, the contractor, the laborer--men in every walk of life--depend for their success upon bringing others to believe, in certain instances, as they believe. Everywhere men who can point out what is right and best, and can bring others to see it and act upon it, win the day.

Another benefit to be obtained from the study of argumentation is the ability to be convinced intelligently. The good arguer is not likely to be carried away by specious arguments or fallacious reasoning. He can weigh every bit of evidence; he can test the strength and weakness of every statement; he can separate the essential from the unessential; and he can distinguish between prejudice and reason. A master of the art of argumentation can both present his case convincingly to others, and discover the truth in a matter that is presented to him.

Argumentation can hardly be considered as a distinct art standing by itself; it is rather a composite of several arts, deriving its fundamentals from them, and depending upon them for its existence. In the first place, since argumentation is spoken or written discourse, it belongs to rhetoric, and the rules which govern composition apply to it as strongly as to any other kind of expression.

In fact, perhaps rhetorical principles should be observed in argumentation more rigidly than elsewhere, for in the case of narration, description, or exposition, the reader or hearer, in an endeavor to derive pleasure or profit, is seeking the author, while in argumentation it is the author who is trying to force his ideas upon the audience. Hence an argument must contain nothing crude or repulsive, but must be attractive in every detail.

In the second place, any composition that attempts to alter beliefs must deal with reasons, and the science of reasoning is logic. There is no need for the student of argumentation to make an exhaustive study of this science, for the good arguer is not obliged to know all the different ways the mind may work; he must, however, know how it should work in order to produce trustworthy results, and to the extent of teaching correct reasoning, argumentation includes logic.

In the third place, a study of the emotions belongs to argumentation. According to the definition, argumentation aims both at presenting truth and compelling action. As action depends to a great extent upon man's emotions, the way to arouse his feelings and passions is a fundamental principle of this art. Argumentation, then, which is commonly classified as the fourth division of rhetoric, consists of two fundamental elements.

The part that is based upon logic and depends for its effectiveness upon pure reasoning is called – conviction -; the part that consists of an emotional appeal to the people addressed is called – persuasion - .

If the only purpose of argumentation were to demonstrate the truth or falsity of a hypothesis, conviction alone would be sufficient. But its purpose is greater than this: it aims both (1) to convince men that certain ideas are true, and also (2) to persuade them to act in accordance with the truth presented. Neither conviction nor persuasion can with safety be omitted.

An appeal to the intellect alone may demonstrate principles that cannot be refuted; it may prove beyond a doubt that certain theories are logical and right, and ought to be accepted. But this sort of argument is likely to leave the person addressed cold and unmoved and unwilling to give up his former ideas and practices.

A purely intellectual discourse upon the evils resulting from a high tariff would scarcely cause a life-long protectionist to change his politics. If, however, some emotion such as duty, public spirit, or patriotism were aroused, the desired action might result.

Again it frequently happens that before the arguer can make any appeal to the logical faculties of those he wishes to influence, he will first have to use persuasion in order to gain their attention and to arouse their interest either in himself or in his subject.

On the other hand, persuasion alone is undoubtedly of even less value than conviction alone.

A purely persuasive argument can never be trusted to produce lasting effects. As soon as the emotions have cooled, if no reasonable conviction remains to guide future thought and action, the plea that at first seemed so powerful is likely to be forgotten.

The preacher whose sermons are all persuasion may, for a time, have many converts, but it will take something besides emotional ecstasy to keep them "in good and regular standing."

The proportion of conviction and persuasion to be used in any argumentative effort depends entirely upon the attending circumstances. If the readers or hearers possess a high degree of intelligence and education, conviction should predominate; for it is a generally accepted fact that the higher man rises in the scale of civilization, the less he is moved by emotion.

A lawyer's argument before a judge contains little except reasoning; before a jury persuasion plays an important part.

In the next place, the arguer must consider the attitude of those whom he would move. If they are favorably disposed, he may devote most of his time to reasoning; if they are hostile, he must use more persuasion. Also the correct proportion varies to some extent according to the amount of action desired.

In an intercollegiate debate where little or no action is expected to result, persuasion may almost be neglected; but the political speech or editorial that urges men to follow its instructions usually contains at least as much persuasion as conviction.

The aspirant for distinction in argumentation should study and acquire certain characteristics common to all good arguers. First of all, he should strive to gain the ability to analyze.

No satisfactory discussion can ever take place until the contestants have picked the question to pieces and discovered just exactly what it means. The man who does not analyze his subject is likely to seize upon ideas that are merely connected with it, and fail to find just what is involved by the question as a whole. The man skillful in argumentation, however, considers each word of the proposition in the light of its definition, and only after much thought and study decides that he has found the real meaning of the question.

But the work of analysis does not end here; every bit of proof connected with the case must be analyzed that its value and its relation to the matter in hand may be determined. Many an argument is filled with what its author thought was proof, but what, upon close inspection, turns out to be mere assertion or fallacious reasoning.

This error is surpassed only by the fault of bringing in as proof that which has no direct bearing at all upon the question at issue.

Furthermore, the arguer must analyze not only his own side of the discussion but also the work of his opponent, so that with a full knowledge of what is strong and what is weak he may make his attack to the best advantage.

Next to the ability to analyze, the most important qualification for an arguer to possess is the faculty of clearly presenting his case.

New ideas, new truths are seldom readily accepted, and it is never safe to assume that the hearer or the reader of an argument will laboriously work his way through a mass of obscure reasoning.

Absolute clearness of expression is essential. The method of arriving at a conclusion should be so plain that no one can avoid seeing what is proved and how it is proved. Lincoln's great success as a debater was due largely to his clearness of presentation.

In the third place, the person who would control his fellow men must assume qualities of leadership. Remembering that men can be led, but seldom be driven, he must show his audience how he himself has reached certain conclusions, and then by leading them along the same paths of reasoning, bring them to the desired destination.

If exhortation, counsel, and encouragement are required, they must be at his command. Moreover, a leader who wishes to attract followers must be earnest and enthusiastic. The least touch of insincerity or indifference will ruin all.

To analyze ideas, to present them clearly, and as a leader to enforce them enthusiastically and sincerely are necessary qualities for every arguer.

A debater should possess additional attainments. He ought to be a ready thinker. The disputant who depends entirely upon a set speech is greatly handicapped. Since it is impossible to tell beforehand just what arguments an opponent will use and what line of attack he will pursue, the man who cannot mass his forces to meet the requirements of the minute is at great disadvantage.

Of course all facts and ideas must be mastered beforehand, but unless one is to be the first speaker, he can most effectually determine during the progress of the debate just what arguments are preferable and what their arrangement should be.

A debater must also have some ability as a speaker. He need not be graceful or especially fluent, though these accomplishments are of service, but he must be forceful. Not only his words, but also his manner must reveal the earnestness and enthusiasm he feels.

His argument, clear, irrefutable, and to the point, should go forth in simple, burning words that enter into the hearts and understanding of his hearers." (end of quoted excerpt)

**

As we have seen, debating is a worthwhile activity for students to learn. It does not matter what occupation a student may eventually choose as a career path. We can say with absolute and total certainty that debating will be useful throughout the entire course of someone's lifetime.

I have presented this information as a *voice from the past*. I strongly believe that every debate coach should be clear about debating as an enriching experience for participants. If this is the case, the debate coach will be a source of enthusiasm and motivation for students to emulate.

As is often the case, and rightfully so, students' attitudes towards, and enjoyment of, any activity is directly influenced by the leadership of the teacher. In this case, the debate coach is responsible for providing the kind of leadership that clearly demonstrates to students that learning to debate is a great investment in their future that will provide many positive returns.

This book has shown examples from contemporary times, and times gone by, of how knowledge gained in debating can be applied practically to the lives of ourselves (debate coach) and our students. Long after the last debate is finished, the positive effects of debating will linger on in our lives.

If we truly desire to make a better world, debating provides us with a possibility to equip our students with the necessary capacity to enter into constructive dialogue with people whom we may disagree with. The more we are able to do this, the more likely we will move towards a world that can live in peace with those whom we have differences of opinion.

Finally, no matter how or why you became a debate coach, you can make a difference. After the initial shock wears off from suddenly becoming the new Debate Society coach, you can begin to use this book to help you recruit, train and establish a positive debating program at your school. Above all, if nothing else, recognise the transformative potential of debate, and provide a positive learning experience for your students. Everything else will ultimately take care of itself...

**

APPENDIX

DEBATE MOTIONS:

This House Believes That...

1. teachers can be replaced by robots.

2. students should not have to take tests.

3. all nuclear weapons should be destroyed.

4. marijuana should be legalized.

5. teenagers should have a midnight curfew.

6. beauty contests for teenagers should be banned.

7. teenagers should be allowed to drive at age 14.

8. boxing should be banned.

9. the United Nations should be abolished.

10. the death penalty should be banned world wide.

11. animals should not be used for sport or entertainment.

12. all genetically modified food should be banned.

13. all people should be required to be organ donors.

14. art is more important than science.

ABOUT THE AUTHOR

Thomas Baker is the Past-President of TESOL Chile (2010-2011). He is the Coordinator of the English Department at Colegio Internacional SEK in Santiago, Chile.

He is the Co-Founder and Co-Organiser of EdCamp Santiago: free, participant-driven, democratic, conversation based professional development for teachers, by teachers. EdCamp Santiago 2013 was held at Universidad UCINF in Santiago.

Thomas is also a past member of the Advisory Board for the International Higher Education Teaching and Learning Association (HETL), where he also serves as a reviewer and as the HETL Ambassador for Chile.
http://hetl.org/ambassador-corps/

Thomas enjoys writing about a wide variety of topics. He has written the following genres: romance, historical fiction, autobiographical, sports history/biography, and English Language Teaching.

https://www.amazon.com/author/thomasjeromebaker

http://www.profesorbaker.com

email: profesorbaker@gmail.com

Twitter: @profesortbaker

Printed in Great Britain
by Amazon.co.uk, Ltd.,
Marston Gate.